EARTHQUAKE

DAILY

❈

EARTHQUAKE

DAILY

✽

JACQUELINE LYONS

NEW MICHIGAN PRESS
TUCSON, ARIZONA

NEW MICHIGAN PRESS
DEPT OF ENGLISH, P. O. BOX 210067
UNIVERSITY OF ARIZONA
TUCSON, AZ 85721-0067

<http://newmichiganpress.com>

Orders and queries to <nmp@thediagram.com>.

Copyright © 2017 by Jacqueline Lyons.
All rights reserved.

ISBN 978-1-934832-64-6. FIRST PRINTING.

Printed in the United States of America.

Design by Ander Monson.

Cover images courtesy of the author.

## CONTENTS

Thursday's Quake  1
Friday's Quake  3
Saturday's Quake  5
Sunday's Quake  7
Monday's Quake  9
Tuesday's Quake  11
Wednesday's Quake  13
Yesterday's Quake  15
Morning Quake  17
Afternoon Quake  19
Night Quake  21
Seven Year Quake  23
Epoch Quake  25
Subconscious Quake  27
Blue Quake  28
Half Quake  30
Second Quake Today  31
Dissolving Quake  33
Advice Quake  34
Unconditional Love Quake  36
August Quake  38

*Acknowledgments*  41

## THURSDAY'S QUAKE

Thursday's quake was centered in personal pronouns, out of our hands and into the hands of giants wandering west-northwest of the civic center shaking residents' beds, according to the U.S. Geological Survey

A seismologist called it "terrifying," and drank bottled water

The quake likely would be studied as an end to the earthquake drought, as a signal of an end, and as a possibility

LA police and seven officials said there were no immediate reports of fireworks from citizens pressing fists to eyelids

Resident Andrea Smith described going into the violent movement as a "considerable breaking" that "trembled her dog"

A neighbor who didn't know what to do with his hands said, "I never could get the hang of Thursdays"

The quake was felt as far off as cursive, as the earth immovable, and words trailing roots with soil still attached, "consider" with stars intact

Broadcasters live on the air stopped time and traveled to separate deserts to be released into a flood of vast personal memories

The quake was typical for how one motorist experienced the shaking alone, while another was certain everyone felt the quake with her.

## FRIDAY'S QUAKE

Today's quake was centered in betrayal, which was preferable to being ignored, said the USGS

"Alaska," offered a seismologist in a tiny office, thinking of the remote park with no entrance, and opened a can of imported salmon

The quake would probably be packed and unpacked, folded and unfolded, buoyed and collapsed, attributing intention without changing the content

Resident Andreas Santi reported being unable to shake an image of a hand held behind a back, fingers closing and unclosing

Other residents described feeling "terrible," and then tried to tell themselves, "It's okay to feel this"

Babies who were honestly crying, and comforted with "Let's go shopping," cried harder, and harder still when wet from the wasted water of tears

Reports of aftershocks appeared and kept appearing, during which someone did some science, and others studied the benefits of occasional paranoid fantasies like someone hiding in their closet waiting for them to come home

It is likely that in the coming weeks city officials will look into eco-loneliness—the latest and oldest of its kind—and the habit of covering the world in leather instead of putting on a pair of shoes.

## SATURDAY'S QUAKE

Saturday the earth shook and was going to shake

The quake centered in heat, and a vision of paper as wood, wood as rock, and the rock on fire, according to the USGS

A seismologist's palms sweated against a sandwich transported by Styrofoam made of heat

Small fires broke out across the region from diaries too hot to handle, reported LA police and other officials, "not only the tiny gold locks," they said "but the syllables themselves conflagrate"

One resident who couldn't stop shaking said, "I can't stop shaking"

Another resident surrounded by air and light described a process by which green plants and some other organisms use sunlight to synthesize foods from carbon dioxide and water, generating oxygen

The quake was unusual for how keenly it illuminated the distance between gold and silver, silver and bronze, bronze and lead

The quake likely would be studied by non-believers who believed in many things, like water and trees as analogous to heart and lungs, and how a landscape's beauty is determined by the rock (bone) beneath

Near the epicenter, crews searched the ground for slight depressions suitable for curling up and lying down in

News agencies received scattered reports of people voluntarily inverting, "to make the ground become the sky, and to replace the sky with ground"

Scientists traveling in a van toward the hot horizon observed the road turn to water, and the water evaporate into air.

## SUNDAY'S QUAKE

Today's quake was centered in fascination with variety among human beings, their ruined bellies, and those beach chairs with individual umbrellas attached

What was unusual was a new alertness to the range of bougainvillea colors that had always been present

The quake would likely be studied for how it affected the pulse, said a seismologist, and for how it affected the sense of a solid earth, said a pulsologist

"People are very different," the USGS reported at a news conference, looking at portraits of Salvador Dali, Gertrude Stein, and Crazy Horse

One resident with an eye color hard to discern said her mode of packing for a day at the beach or for an emergency was "to bring as much as possible," while another said she told her kids "the opposite," then looked around for approval

The quake was typical for how quickly people got used to the shaking, and how they voted to suffer separately instead of gathering together in the town hall

The quake struck approximately ten minutes after the customer service industry decided to replace the human voice with a computer-generated one

And was felt as far to the north as the street you didn't grow up on called Floating Cloud, and as far to the south as a woman turning away from her children and the ocean to look at her phone.

## MONDAY'S QUAKE

Monday's quake was centered in a sudden lightness after letting go, as when a tug of war rope slips free, or one lets herself cross an invisible line

Monday was National Break-up Day, so most residents found themselves alone in their cars when the temblor struck, following a double or single or solid or dotted line

A geologist with the USGS spoke of the vertical narrative told by a giant crack in the earth, and how his hands float up after he sets down his bags

The quake came as a shock to those at the epicenter, though friends in neighboring areas reported being "not surprised"

The quake would likely be studied for how it made morning coffee taste "different" and "not in a bad way," said a seismologist surfing the web, who decided to let go of Monday

Monday's quake had been rehearsed frequently in the mind before finally being enacted, and even then from inside the anonymity of a uniform

Some outside the seismic zone reported envy, though officials said these individuals would probably stay where they were, because "better the devil you know"

There were no reports of structural damage or physical injury, though the local DJ's morning play list included what one official identified as "empowering break-up songs"

Resident Sandra Smith said the quake felt like "a weight lifted from my shoulders," then quickly revised it to "a weight lifted from my chest," and demonstrated with several deep breaths, each envisioned as pure white light on the inhale, and gray smoke on the exhale

The quake was felt as far to the north as a solo visit to an amusement park, and as far to the south as a road trip on highways without dividing lines.

## TUESDAY'S QUAKE

Tuesday's quake was centered in 90% of seabirds discovered to have plastic in their stomachs

The quake struck between Monday and Friday, so most residents were stuck in traffic, fire raining from the sky

The chance of anyone forming new neural pathways or being okay with Tuesday as simultaneously a lucky and an unlucky day appeared "somewhat small," said officials, trying to pat their heads and rub their tummies while putting on oxygen masks

The quake left one seismologist, descended from saints, with a new appreciation for the paradoxical vibration of "seabird"

A resident who had recently moved to the area from a quiet place on earth said the quake reminded her of when she was a girl and islands floated on the ocean like breaching whales, a time when "it was good, it was good"

Scientists are attempting to calculate the energy required to digest unsaid words, and how some residents' mouths seem unable to form the words "sorry" and "mistake"

Aftershocks were reported in the form of residents resting one hand on their rising and falling diaphragms, the other fluttering to their throats

Neighbors who crossed the threshold to introduce themselves to sky for the first time found themselves warmed by the blue-black light of crows flying inland for the evening.

## WEDNESDAY'S QUAKE

Wednesday's quiet quake was centered and rippling a few miles east or west of precarious equanimity, according to the USGS

"Who knows how long it will last," said a seismologist, pushing up her glasses in a habitual gesture

Moments before the temblor struck, residents near the epicenter gave up balancing on one foot and sat down to put on the other shoe

A spokesperson for those who were awake observed, "most people don't know what their house is built upon," and then announced she was taking a lower paying job somewhere free from the terror of commuter traffic

What was unusual about the quake was how no one called it terrible, and the sound it made, which resembled olive leaves growing heavy with moisture from being slowly flown over vast water through fog

Resident Drew Tanis was paddle boarding somewhere on the thinning and spreading earth when the quake struck, planting in his mind the word "terrain," and convincing him that the opposite of peace is unhappiness, and the opposite of happiness is the Santa Ana aka "devil" winds

The quake would likely be studied as an example of how difficult it is to acquire "the wisdom to know the difference," said a geologist practicing tree pose on a slack line, and for how not enough sleep is okay until it isn't

By the time cotyledon petals relaxed, uncertainty was already underway in the form of a box wind at a hot air balloon rally, the uneven field beneath, and coffee sloshing dangerously in a single use cup

In the north, residents experienced an acute sense of the ovoid earth, and in the south, worry over money turned to worry over water and could no longer be contained.

## YESTERDAY'S QUAKE

The quake struck during 47% of our waking hours when we were thinking about something other than what was actually happening right now

"What's done is done," said a USGS geologist, holding up a heather gray rock erupting with white starbursts from strong impacts, and "events in the field of awareness"

Several residents taking the same night class reported glimpses of thoughts as clouds drifting across a sky, as leaves flowing by in a stream, and as images flickering on a screen

Was the field below the clouds alongside the stream seeded with daffodils, safflower, or winter wheat?

While one resident tried to recall when he had last occupied the present moment, a hawk swooped in and killed a dove on the roof of a business school

"It is what it is," said a resident and working poet who was beginning to get the hang of her one and only life

Tomorrow's quake will most likely be centered in today, and trying to keep the spotlight of attention from sliding off the soles of the feet, said someone whose name we forget

What was unusual about this quake was a growing interest in where thoughts reside, and the origins of a dream in which we unfold a map and find ourselves surrounded by a sea or very great lake

Aftershocks arrived in the form of an image of snowflakes fluttering inside a capacious dome when asked, "what's on your mind."

Seismologists with the USGS would be monitoring our warped amygdalae, which vibrate as if tigers encircle us whenever we think of what our boss said yesterday, or tomorrow's traffic, or love without guarantee.

## MORNING QUAKE

A daybreak-truncating quake shortly after dawn today replaced wide-eyed morning with chain saw, with broken, with leaf blower and abbrev

Numinous residents have been reporting threats to wide-eyed morning for at least 12 years—attacks on shine, dreams saddled, threshold bridges collapsed

"Everything is a poem," sang a resident of seven continents, equally at home everywhere, gazing at a shovel glazed with smog—then a backhoe interrupted

Seismologists with the USGS said they would be closely monitoring those still connected to wide-eyed morning, vibrations felt by bare feet in the kitchen, by claws in the sand, and tone when greeting a toad discovered to have spent the night inside

The quake was felt as far to the north as the frayed hem of a bulb's skirt of light, and as far to the south as mistaking the temporary for the permanent

Mind colonizing quakes had happened before, and would probably happen again every week day about this time unless—

"I've never really felt part and parcel of wide-eyed morning before," said a geologist, driving his van really fast, hoping to blur different species of trees into one clonal grove

"Wide-eyed morning's undeniable rhythms," explained a seismologist with a rich interior life, pressing her ear to the ground

Like a bird coming down the walk, except the ground made of water, the bird born of light

Officials who were in the habit of not listening to other officials agreed that the wide-eyed morning newscaster's voice echoed earth's blue rolling motion.

## AFTERNOON QUAKE

A late afternoon quake was centered in the girl you were, taken out so early and shot along with an unnamed beagle, cats enraptured by birds, wild turkeys, pretty skunks, opossums who suffer too, and, yearly, one shy deer

"Can you feel empathy for that girl?" asked Dr. Aneas, her curly hair unruly inside the tiny office

We nodded Yes, having suffered the backs of our thighs sticking to plastic couches

The epicenter was seated in the denial of unconditional love, and our little dog threatened, too

"Most of us lack a prescription for mourning the living," said a USGS seismologist monitoring catastrophe thousands of miles away from the mouth of a cave

The quake was felt as far to the west as the unwilding effect of "whoa!" shouted to a girl swinging high, and as far to the east as scolded for running to the edge of the circumference

Aftershocks were reported in the form of liquefying silence that followed an invitation to "think of someone who loves you deeply"

Residents who volunteered to help themselves were counseled to go out and get their girl whatever she wants

The quake registered on the dominant hand as a four-point-not-the-worst-childhood-ever, and on the other hand as an eight-point-you'll-never-get-another-one

One resident, an adult, stood in the blue shadow of fracture and thought he heard promises by the sea beneath or the sea within for an improved infancy, and dove in to find it

Officials said a lot of things we should probably cast off as inner parental voices, and instead get the haircut, ruby slippers, pet bunny, or five-string banjo we always wanted

And the vibrations, the vibrations, the vibrations

Geologists seemed hopeful that the split earth would swallow the four-legged that rose up monstrous onto two in recurring childhood dreams, and put it to bed once and for all.

## NIGHT QUAKE

A night quake radiated from the rapid construction of a very long wall, from monetary recompense for wrongful death, from failure to save a burning forest

"A wall might keep something out, or keep something in," observed just about anyone seven or older with a little imagination

"I love my walls," said one resident, lucky to be born a resident

Aftershocks were reported as coins stacked vertebrae-like then crashed, shattered, lights put out

Foreshocks had arrived in the form of offers to buy land from people whose only home on earth was their land, including its trees, dead and alive

The epicenter was located in no longer justifiable fears, and failure to notice the direction of prevailing winds

The disparity between the sense of a unified landscape as seen from the air and the sharp division felt on the ground when trying to walk a straight line home after dark immobilized some residents, whose fists clenched and unclenched at their sides

Other residents reported being unable to discern up from down, "which is ironic in an era of renewed binary opposition," said a geologist who spent a lot of time on the trembling ground

One young person whose life mattered had forced upon her the resemblance between chain link fences when met with force, and many shots fired simultaneously into the dark

Dark, darker, darkest

The quake struck in the dead of night, which some nations argued was midnight, the bewitching hour, when form unlooses and stones exhale, while others insisted it was the hour before dawn when it is always darkest and a torn sky lowers a gray jagged seam.

## SEVEN YEAR QUAKE

This year's quake was centered in the body seven years ago replaced by the body now

"One body makes us think of another, and a giant crack in the earth makes our sentences long," said a resident on earth, lifting a vessel with her heart, opening windows with her lungs, and shouldering burdens, cell by cell by cell by cell

"If we breathe, we are alive, and if we are alive, all things are possible," said a geologist with the USGS who celebrates Ground Hog Day every day, "we don't tend to think of it this way"

And eyes moving in their orbits, hip joints rotating in their sockets

Resident Endrasa Stein, who stood a short distance away from her body when the quake unfolded, told reporters "Emergency is emergency is emergency is emergency"

The quake struck in evening as tenor and vehicle thinned to breaking, the dying stars not resembling carbon turning crystalline beneath the ground

The quiet mind-blowing quake caused shaking on a cellular level, and generated the most imagery since the news that the majority of the human body is composed of water

The epicenter was located in the vicinity of happy hour, where four out of five trivia questions were answered correctly while only half-listening and eating fish tacos: Genesis, the Galapagos, the Dalai Lama, Frida Kahlo

Eye, neighbor to ear, into heart, becomes breath

A Utah seismologist and divorcee who identified as a widow walked out of her office, down the hall, past the café and into the atrium where she looked past a skeleton displayed inside its glass case and forward to meeting her newest body.

## EPOCH QUAKE

This epoch's quake was centered in a figurative "no man's land" becoming literal

But striking us maybe more so as "no woman's land", said a seismologist and single mom whose child was fathered and abandoned by a surrealist, "and more of a sad land, not unlike a badland"

And being guided away, guided and guided away

When asked whether they presumed USGS geologists to be women or men, officials admitted they always pictured men, ones who looked a lot like them

One resident, who had "no idea" that people were falling through the cracks, had not yet peered into the sink hole in his backyard

Another resident, who hoped to see steps taken toward retrofitting before more disastrous phrases were uttered, turned blue at the throat and chose not to speak

"I had a dream that stress in the outer earth built until rocks slipped and sent waves traveling through the earth's crust" shared a seismologist with the USGS, "and then there was a buffet of dark chocolate cakes and cherries, but I couldn't taste them"

The unarmed and unidentified speculated that the quake would strike and keep striking until we learned to really look at someone, to touch with our eyes a person named Mel

The quake was felt as far away as a girl steered clear of numbers' clean lines by comments made about the body beneath her dress

Though many temblors have struck the region since earthquake recording began, none has been strong enough to vibrate moon and sun from their separate skies, said city officials in a statement

Outside a border, in rainy no man's land, stood children, women and men with warm palms, bad kidneys and thin shirts, craving a giant hand to curl up in.

## SUBCONSCIOUS QUAKE

Somewhere a quake was centered in the tail end of last
   night's dream slipping out of reach
      and water, water everywhere

You don't believe half of it anyway, or yourself
      you believe a thread when it leads back to its nest

You seize the syllables in "flotsam" and "jetsam"
      though with elephantine pull toward a mother heart land

What washes up on dry land loses its given name
      morning finds sweetness emptied, terribly

In some worlds, thoughts go flying leaping into the waves, lope back
   bright-eyed
      in some minds, ideas shoot like a bullet, lodged, spent

Some men are mice, ignore the wheel for a crumb
      forest destroyed, then they know a tree

In which world and body did someone last surprise you—not me—
      by guessing correctly, exactly—and make you believe

Holding up their end even as the ship
      skids and flies off the road.

## BLUE QUAKE

No one is here
    where brown turns blue and back again
where soil spins a sphere you wake and put your shoulder to

You are most like the transverse fault whose shadow you lie down in
    when you go to the zoo or zoo-like tavern
stare and stare, then pound
    your fist on the glass, once, before returning to the trees

The sun does not rise but shines while the earth circles
    coyote-like, submitting to light

You have a hat that may contain you, a belt to cinch
    around that which you tell in the blue black night, "you can go now"

No one to miss, no one to witness
    a moving truck slip between cracks at midnight
except a moose who didn't turn from his browsing

It's one rare bird who can weather the seasons on a single branch

Those first boys/men, their necks smelled cobalt, their throats up close
    the color of pure air

Where did all this space come from—distancing you
    from postcards that began "Hello Beautiful"

You exited for the view and the rest of the herd moved on
    while you looked around, they counted you lost

If only you knew then, once, what you've now learned at least twice

The earth is not a perfect sphere, there's a season for mating,
    blue light is everything but.

## HALF QUAKE

If today were a quake it would center in unable
    to mirror the color of no trouble

If today were a color, coral
    of hot sunrise in September, dog days gone on too long,
    feeling like forever

If today's heart were a dog's, it would beat erratic

If today sustained an injury, it would be to the spine
    preventable, inevitable, straight out of the earth in
    a bruised time

Today's plan—in the skeletal stages

In today's bony hand a sign: Prepare to Stop

If today were a string it would be attached
    by barbed wire or barbed threads and with thready pulse
    to the past's tarnished glass.

## SECOND QUAKE TODAY

One quake after another was triggered by rounds of complimentary chardonnay on a delayed Alaskan Airways flight out of Burbank

And by clouds nerved and sheathed, clouds dark and branching

Quakes swarmed the ambiguity of "anchorage," one weight dropped, one horizon settled upon

You decide you could marry the man at the Anchorage restaurant who handed you the menu upright—his flannel, his plaid, his pupils wide in summer

Because what is more secure than a home in winter, more confusing than land liquefied, more mixed than being cut from a wedding dress night after night

And the seafood stew he recommended—you could eat it with a fork

You would not return to the 7th floor of an Anchorage hotel after a week on the Marine Highway, the room pitched and swayed like the wrong drink the bartender crushed

You wanted a Manhattan, not Old Fashioned, though yes to the cherry glow and colorful locals, you might have loved them if you had known, might have identified in the clouds a lamp, a toothbrush, a library book, a whale

The last man you travelled with across the earth's surface—hatless, vested, some fun cocktails together but too dinner knife in the right hand, not enough undressed

In the middle of a glacier he was dessert plates on the table foreshadowing, you could see from miles away that the scene would fail to transmogrify.

## DISSOLVING QUAKE

Today's quake centered in a place that belongs to its green proliferations, not to us
    a place that doesn't look like it used to, or hear its real name
        the south fork of a River hears itself called "Creek"

a creek that moves like a creek except faster, over more rocks, inside a weather like the weather except
hotter and hotter   ice that doesn't remember
        a memory but not ours
                us but in separate strands, hotter and with

more constraints
    constraints that could surface thick veins of ore except when they limit
        our and the creek's freedom limited by word count by
bumper stickers by re-naming by private beaches, and flags
                flags slowing the forward movement of trucks
and shadowing restaurant parking lots
        except one flag, right now, near this creek, flag-like except

peaceful, carrying itself away—

## ADVICE QUAKE

Today's quake centered in a tree's advice to "let go"

The tree is also going to need us to shake out our shoulders and soften our faces

And to learn its names, its many names

The quake struck in late afternoon, a time of roadside trees blurred by speeding cars, trees that need us to listen into the noise, the many noises, for the edges of sounds

A geologist in one quadrant of the tangle kept an ear to the ground, listening for the rock's side of the story, a song about the disappearance of song, a song that is going to need us to sing for her

One resident, dazzled by light, walked right into a web strung between trees, then marveled at how muscles in her mouth and throat worked together to shape a small scream

The quake was felt as far to the north as hair falling into our eyes, again, and as far to the south as having heard this advice before, of course we have heard it before

The quake's epicenter hovered over the sexiness of "I'm going to need you"

The quake would likely be studied for how nonjudgmental we feel when entering a grove where one or more aspens have gathered

Too many kinds of advice to name, such as acacia, apple, ash, birch, catalpa, cedar, chestnut, cottonwood, cypress, eucalyptus, ficus, fir, hemlock, ironwood, juniper, linden, maple, oak, olive, palm, pine, redwood, sequoia, sycamore.

## UNCONDITIONAL LOVE QUAKE

*for Macchia*

An early morning quake vibrates the earth west-southwest of
    the bed's shoreline
caused by the dog's first-thing-in-the-morning dance

the sea calls her
the ocean calls louder
the full moon tugs at her collar

inside her third eyelid an incoming tide washes up a vision of
    beds and bacon-flavored treats, of low couches made of wool
    and fleece scattered with peanut butter treats, cushions to
    laze upon and run in place while asleep

in washes a thought: live long enough to tire of couches, surpass
    sand and salt
and put bare belly to the duck-flavored waves

this is what she says with her two-steps-forward-one-step-back
    and cresting whine
this and that she needs to go outside

morning has arrived, and brings with it an open door, a full
    bowl
so she waltzes her ebb and flow

the sea swells in her wet nose
the tide ripples through her spine
the moon fades fast in the west

she sends me a message in a bottle
by pressing her seal-fur-forehead to mine
"Wake up and taste the salmon-colored sky."

## AUGUST QUAKE

Today's quake was centered in summer's end, in flowers dissolving their fireworks back to a single stem

"We've no reason to be surprised," said USGS beneath a moon sharpening her horn

Residents near the epicenter witnessed sprawling highway mirages evaporate into dotted lines

In aftershocks, calendar squares circled the wagons separating grasshoppers from ants

City officials with mild hands and weakness for euphemism speculated, "summer would want us to celebrate not mourn her passing"

A peace trainer wondered which was sadder—to tear down your own web every evening, or capitulate it to the night

Southern California seismologists paused to choose their words carefully before commenting on the logic and heat generated from arms folded across the chest

Icelandic seismologists who had all winter to reflect said you couldn't pay them to move away from giant green lights streaking across the sky

One resident endured a personal aftershock of exponential magnitude triggered by her father never looking at her, or her sisters, or mother as if they were beautiful and precious flowers

A dog adopted at the end of summer forgets all other summers, every day dissolves its reflection by drinking from the fish pond

A dog brought to closing night of the free outdoor Shakespeare festival watches flowering vines thin to power cords during the final soliloquy, charms all o'erthrown

"Where could you go that's not already gone," say mourning doves to each other tightening their belts, and "better to have never summered at all."

## ACKNOWLEDGMENTS

Thank you to the editors and staff of the journals in which some of the poems first appeared: *Interim*, for "Morning Quake," "Friday's Quake," and "Sunday's Quake;" *Salamander*, for "Epoch Quake," "Seven Year Quake," and "Second Quake Today."

Thank you to seismologist Katherine Whidden for our conversation on earthquakes, poetry, and Murakami. Thank you to staff at Carrizo Plain National Monument, and Parkfield Lodge and Café. Thank you to California Lutheran University for a Faculty Research and Creative Work Award that supported the research and writing of these poems, and to my colleagues at CLU who generously shared earthquake news and stories. Gratitude to Sherwin Bitsui, Peter Covino, Heather Winterer, Justin Hocking, and Chris Cokinos for reading early versions of these poems. And thank you to John, the best quake.

JACQUELINE LYONS is the author of the poetry collections *The Way They Say Yes Here* (Hanging Loose Press), which won a Peace Corps Writers Best Poetry Book Award, *Lost Colony* (Dancing Girl Press), the nonfiction manuscript *Breakdown of Poses*, which was a finalist for the AWP Award Series Prize in Creative Nonfiction, and a new poetry collection forthcoming in 2018 from Barrow Street Press. She is Associate Professor of English and Creative Writing at California Lutheran University, and lives on the southern segment of the San Andreas fault.

✺

COLOPHON

Text is set in a digital version of Jenson, designed by Robert Slimbach in 1996, and based on the work of punchcutter, printer, and publisher Nicolas Jenson. The titles here are in Futura.

❉

NEW MICHIGAN PRESS, based in Tucson, Arizona, prints poetry and prose chapbooks, especially work that transcends traditional genre. Together with DIAGRAM, NMP sponsors a yearly chapbook competition.

DIAGRAM, a journal of text, art, and schematic, is published bimonthly at THEDIAGRAM.COM. Periodic print anthologies are available from the New Michigan Press at NEWMICHIGANPRESS.COM.

www.ingramcontent.com/pod-product-compliance
Lightning Source LLC
Chambersburg PA
CBHW031505040426
42444CB00007B/1213